# Messages From The Divine Mother

A Selection of Spiritual Conversations For Women

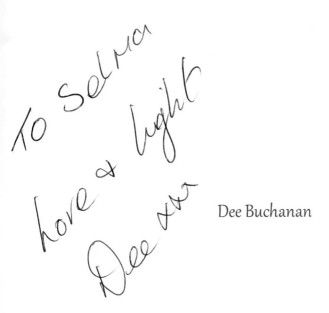

To Selma
love & light
Dee xx

Dee Buchanan

**BALBOA**.PRESS

A DIVISION OF HAY HOUSE

Balboa Press books may be ordered through booksellers or by contacting:

Balboa Press
A Division of Hay House
1663 Liberty Drive
Bloomington, IN 47403
www.balboapress.co.uk
UK TFN: 0800 0148647 (Toll Free inside the UK)
UK Local: (02) 0369 56325 (+44 20 3695 6325 from outside the UK)

Because of the dynamic nature of the Internet, any web addresses or links contained in this book may have changed since publication and may no longer be valid. The views expressed in this work are solely those of the author and do not necessarily reflect the views of the publisher, and the publisher hereby disclaims any responsibility for them.

The author of this book does not dispense medical advice or prescribe the use of any technique as a form of treatment for physical, emotional, or medical problems without the advice of a physician, either directly or indirectly. The intent of the author is only to offer information of a general nature to help you in your quest for emotional and spiritual well-being. In the event you use any of the information in this book for yourself, which is your constitutional right, the author and the publisher assume no responsibility for your actions.

Any people depicted in stock imagery provided by Getty Images are models, and such images are being used for illustrative purposes only. Certain stock imagery © Getty Images.

Print information available on the last page.

ISBN: 978-1-9822-8523-4 (sc)
ISBN: 978-1-9822-8525-8 (hc)
ISBN: 978-1-9822-8524-1 (e)

Balboa Press rev. date:   03/09/2022

'It is always there…'

"Whenever we need an answer, it is there. No matter what the situation is, our higher self knows exactly what is best for us… No matter how long it has been since we consciously communicated with it, the power within us remains steady… The spirit within us is there for us always. We just have to acknowledge it, praise it, thank it and know everything is all right now."

- **Iyanla Vanzant**, 'Acts of Faith-
Daily Meditations For People Of Colour'

*Dedicated to the Ancestors who paved the way for me to be here. And to all my family and friends who have joined them in the spirit realm.*

# Contents

# Foreword

Messages from the Divine Mother is fundamentally a "doing word" — a verb spiritually metabolised. As it is read, the words transform and are assimilated into energy.

The beautifully crafted messages in this book provide soothing writings from what feels like a pure place, and are able to transcend contexts; these messages are therefore effervescent and ever relevant. It feels like a deep tissue healing balm and the restoration tingles and his verb tingles.

Messages from the Divine Mother provide affirmations that speak to me as a Diaspora daughter of African heritage. I didn't know what I would find, read or receive. I did not have any specific expectations but what I experienced have exceeded my greatest expectations.

Messages from the Divine Mother is a collection of the love notes you would yearn for, from a wise one with only unconditional love for you. It is equivalent to witnessing the blossoming of a sacred and diluted love affair. When I read it, it feels like I'm reading love notes. It opens up chakras, and it balances. It is an incredibly penetrating read. I paused, reflected, and resumed. I gasped; I nodded my head, I smiled. I had epiphanies, I made agreement sounds, and I had experience after experience. This is a healing balm.

I received assurance and reassurance. It provided sustenance. It reinforced the unwavering love of a Most High Mother, granting permission. It must be read. It must be listened to, and it must be shared. It illuminates love. It ignited a neglected yearning to hear the soothing validation of Mother energy.

I want to give it to my daughter, I want my daughter to give it to her daughter, I want to give it to my granddaughter and I want to give it to my niece. I want us all to sit down and talk about it. And even just mother to child and mother energy to our Elders. I can imagine reading this to those who don't even get many visitors or don't hear many voices. Even those people who are not in the same place as you, you know this is transnational, international, outer national work.

I want us to be in spaces where we just say, "Let's reach for Messages from the Divine Mother" and open it. Yes, just open it everywhere we can.

The content within Messages from the Divine Mother is personal. It transcends separation and nations. It is an intimately personal message from the Source through the author to the reader. The author has many strengths and a significant one is humility. Other ones include a sense of service, knowledge of Self and a willingness to learn and share. The one that I want to bring attention to at this time is gentleness. This gentleness is the vehicle for help with a gaping wound in need of care and resolution. The wound is often largely hidden, but yet, affecting the lived experience of the reader. This is important material for those who have experienced trauma and are in recovery. These messages uncover and provide the gateway to healing.

Messages from the Divine Mother is a gift to humanity. It's a tool to take self-development and empowerment to a higher level.

It is an authentic, heart-to-heart, undiluted communication. I have no hesitation in recommending what is now my go to Spirit read to all, but especially women and girls. It is an ideal solitary read, but can also provide reading for friendship circles, preparatory work and centring. I am thrilled to endorse this phenomenal contribution to our healing and spiritual elevation. I look forward to reading further works as you continue to bring your unique perspective to a world in need of you.

Thank you. Alpha, Mother Father God, and you Dee, daughter of The Most High. You come from Mt Zion.

**SisDr Sandra Richards** - Author, Cultural Counsellor, Coach, and Educator.

# Introduction

I'm sitting by the window. The night has just drawn in; it is almost dark. The grey shadows dance with the light. I'm on the floor, eagerly excited to read the book I have just purchased, recommended by my dear friend, Lester Lewis: "Tapping the Power Within" by *Iyanla Vanzant*. I'm excited and fully immersed in the first couple of pages. It was like the book was about me and my struggles in life, and the challenges I have had in recognising who I am. The book spoke about the divinity within me and I wished I could only just reconcile this within myself, and then these words hit me:

*"You should understand that as an African descendant, spirit and spirituality are a wholesome element of your basic nature. You are not replacing or undermining God in developing your spirit, you are trying to make contact with the powerful force that is God within you. What you are seeking and searching for has always been with you."*

Tapping the Power Within, Iyanla Vanzant

My soul opened up to new thoughts, new ways of being and all of a sudden it came like a bolt in my spirit. I knew it to be true.

I knew that the real me had been hidden away in fear of not being accepted, and not loved because I was different. I was afraid to be different. I was afraid that it was not okay to be me. In that lightning bolt moment, I knew that God loved me and accepted me for who I am because I was created in divinity and love.

"Whoa…. I am okay as I am?" This was the question that I kept asking myself, until finally the answer came: Yes! I am okay as I am. I am okay as I am. This is the way God wanted me to be. This is who He wants me to be.

There was a time when I looked outside of myself to find God. I went from church to church, religion to religion, looking for God. I could not find Him out there. Until that night, I did not know that God was within me and has always been there with me. I had been searching for something outside of myself, when all the time it was within me.

I lay the book down and sat there in silence for a while, going over the words that I had just read. My mind was racing, my spirit was racing. I was in a trance-like state, caught up in the revelations of my soul… I knew this to be true because I felt it. Yet, my mind was taking time to assimilate and accommodate this truth.

I got up and laid on my bed, book laying on my chest and stared up at the ceiling thinking over what I had just read. And then, laughter took over... I laughed, laughed and laughed some more. My heart was pouring out with pure joy and laughter and in that moment, there was my friend, Lester, laughing with me as if to say, "I told you- you will find the truth." I laughed and it was as if Lester was laughing with me too. We laughed together even more.

You see, I convinced myself that it was not okay to be me. I have always felt different, but thought my difference was not to be acknowledged. I felt things that others did not feel and saw things that others did not see. I needed to have permission from something or someone outside myself to be me. I now realize that this is me and there is no-one else like me. I want to be Me.

As I lay on my bed, a voice kept repeating to me the words, *"Life Within, Life Within, Life Within."* I could not get the words out of my head, so, I jumped off the bed and grabbed a pen and paper and began to write. Then the first verse came. **"Live from within thy heart."** Then the second verse came through, **"For within thy heart, thy soul takes part."** I was not in control of what I was writing. It was as if something or someone else was telling me what to write. So, I wrote what was coming through without question. I wrote without thought; I just wrote what came through to me. Hence my first spiritual poem was born.

As I looked over the poem, I had no recollection of where the words came from. All I knew and felt was the words coming through me. I reflected on what came through and attempted to sign my name as the Author. I could not. So, I sat with this for a while. It became very apparent that the author of this poem wanted to be known. So, I wrote what I heard —*'Alpha.'*

At the time, I didn't know the true meaning of the name *"Alpha"* but I knew what had occurred was coming from a higher place, a spiritual place. I was given this poem to write. After that night, other poems came through in the same manner; a voice either saying the title or the first sentence came to my mind and the compulsivity to continue to write completely took over any sense of being. It had to be written and then the rest would just follow. It was from there I embarked on my own spiritual journey. I guess this was the start of listening to "The Voice."

Soon after this, I began journaling after attending a writer's workshop. For homework, we were given affirmations to write every morning as the first thing you would do upon waking.

I did this for a while and then I began to write about how I was feeling that day. Over time, my journaling took me to a different level. I began every morning by writing to the Divine Mother.

One morning as I began to write, I heard the voice talking directly to me. **"My Dear Daughter..."** was how it started. I had no control over what I was writing. I wrote what I heard. Whatever I was feeling that day, whatever question I posed, I was given an answer. Guidance, love, empathy, blessings and a lot more all came out on the page. Day after day, this is how I would receive my messages.

Over 20 years of journaling brought these messages into existence. Come to the present moment, the energy of the words and the messages that came through has made me realise that this has to be shared. These messages can help support and empower others – empower women to learn and grow and understand themselves. And so... *"Messages from the Divine Mother"* was born.

# Messages From the Divine Mother

*A Selection of Spiritual Conversations for Women*

Good morning, Mother, I thought that I would start my day by meditating on a thought I woke up with. My feelings this morning is one of optimism that everything will be alright. I woke up this morning with the sun shining and that made a difference.

Oh, Merciful Mother, I have found a place where we can be together. Where I can spend time with you. Oh, Glorious Mother, your daughter of love is calling. The unseen love of the great ones before me is all around me.

I shall wear white today to signify the purity of love and joy of You, Divine Mother and the Ancestors.

Oh, Glorious Holy Ones, how great it is to know you and to love you. How glorious it is to be part of the root.

As a child, I used to question things like, "Why was I born as part of this root (black)?" I know this does not sound like a positive question, but there is a reason for me being born in this root. I am so uplifted to know of the rich heritage that I have been born into. Of the glorious tree of life that I am a branch of. Ancestors of The Most High, I salute you. I salute my divinity.

Oh Mother, is it not glorious to be part of such a heritage? Is it not just wonderful to be a princess growing into a queen? Oh, Merciful Father, Creator of all with your Queen (Mother) beside you. Oh, this is a glorious day for the ancestors and for me as a child of the universe.

Oh, Merciful Mother, you know so much about me that I am still discovering. Oh, Merciful God the Father and God the Mother. I love you. Praise to you The Most High, the glorious, the all-powerful, the all-knowing, the all-wise, the ever loving, the guiding light.

# Life Within

# Life Within

Live from within thy heart.

For within thy heart

Thy soul takes part.

Thy Spirits gather together in glee.

Oh, what a meeting this will be.

Thy Heart, thy Soul and thy Spirit,

are all together

Within Thee.

*Alpha*

My Dear Daughter,

You are the best there is. Don't you think you deserve the best? That's what you have to realise, my dear daughter. You are the best there is. I made you perfect and you are undoing all that Father and I have given you. Shine my daughter, for you are the light, you are the one that we give to the world, the light that shines in darkness.

You know, you know, so shine my love, shine my daughter. That's all we ask of you, to glow in your light.

There is nothing that we cannot help you through.

You only have to ask...

We are here for you.

*You are the best there is — perfect and complete.*

Dearest Daughter,

You are not alone, we are with you. Come out of your haze and darkness and into the light. We are the light, dear daughter. We are bearers of life. We give unto you what there is for you; we are waiting for you my dear daughter. It is all that you deserve, all that you will be and more. You just need to ask and it shall be given unto you.

*We just need to ask!*

We are waiting and have been waiting for your call. Do not be afraid as fear will not bring you the richness that is waiting for you. Come to us with joy, love and peace and we will abundantly supply more than you even dreamed.

*Abundance is always waiting to be claimed.*

You just need to have the faith and the conviction that what we say is true. This is the truth of life.

*Having faith in everything that you do will always bring results.*

Oh, my dear daughter, there is so much that we can tell you but all in good time. There is so much we can show you, but all in good time. Just show us and tell us that you trust us and have faith in us and all will be revealed.

*Trust the process and it will manifest.*

Oh, my dear daughter, we love you so much.

Don't think that we don't know what you are going through. We do. Just promise that you will listen and grow with us all the time.

My dearest daughter, We love you...

*In challenging times, we just need to listen.*

Slow down... Take it easy... I will be with you all day and every day, just call on me. I will not neglect or forget to support you in what you do. I love you, my daughter. I love every part of your being.

Don't despair, everything will be alright.

*Just call on the Divine Mother's Spirit and all will be well.*

You will see this all one day as a stepping stone, a push in the right direction. Don't worry, you are doing fine. You are letting go and letting me in. That can't be bad. All that I ask of you is to let me be your guide.

*Trust the Divine Mother to guide you in the right direction.*

I know you my daughter, more than you know yourself, so let me in, don't shut me out in times of need, I will be there. And in times of Joy, I will be there.

*The Divine Mother is always waiting to be let in.*

I love you; I love you; I love you; you are all that the power is. You are love, beauty peace, joy, all knowing, understanding, strength and health. All that the power is, you are...

One Love...

*Opening the doors of your Spirit is your 'Soul' requirement.*

My daughter, go in peace, my dear loved one.

Make this day a beautiful day and learn something new today. And don't forget to love today.

I honour the divinity in you...Peace my daughter, Peace. One Love... Mother.

*Sometimes all you need is to listen to your Spirit.*

It's all within you to find out. Look within and you will find the truth. It's all there for you, nothing is hidden from you if you truly seek it. All you need is within you.

*Nothing is hidden from within you.*

My daughter, there is no need to fight or beat up on yourself.

You don't need to look outside of yourself, it is all within you.

Right here and right now, always.

*Your answers cannot be found outside, look within.*

My Dear Daughter,

Don't despair, don't worry endlessly, because all the answers are within you. You will have to trust yourself, know yourself and be yourself. That is all you need to do.

*Having faith and trust in yourself is your source of happiness.*

# Love

# Love

Love oneself to know oneself.

Love each other to be together.

Love unconditionally for there is no condition.

Love unlimited for there is no limit.

Love because there is a cause.

Love with emotion for there will be feelings.

Love with feelings for it's the centre of touch.

Love with embrace for it is your security.

Love with God for its your pathway to heaven.

*Alpha*

My Dear Daughter,

I love you too. I have loved you from the day you were created. I have always loved the way you speak, the way you carry yourself and the way you care for others.

*The Divine Mother's love is never conditional.*

I love you, my gentle daughter. I love you for who you are. I love you for who you are Be-in, so unique and wonderful in all things that you do. You are beautiful my daughter, you are wonderful and courageous. Peace be with you today and every day.

One love my daughter... One Love.

*Love is all we need to be.*

I love you, love you, love you. Be at peace with yourself and I will be at peace with you. Be at peace my love. Have faith in me to guide you to success.

*To Thyself Be True.*

My Dear Daughter,

You don't need to share love; you need to give love. Love is what you are. You are love. When you fully understand this, you will realise that you are all that you are, which is love. Then you will meet the love that you are. You will recognise the love that you are.

*Divine Mother's love will always carry you through.*

You recognise the harmony of self-knowing and the love of service that you shared within your own heart. What you did not recognise was the unavailability, the withdrawal, the neediness and the space that you needed. All you have to do is relax, be yourself.

*When the time is ripe, you will be fruitful.*

You will find the true love of your life. But remember, it is you, the real you who they will love. But if you put up a facade then they won't want to know or are afraid of who you really are.

*True love will find its path to you.*

So, in all things, be yourself and don't be who you think they want you to be. In the meantime, relax, breathe, exercise and have fun. Yes, have fun! And laugh…

*Life can be so easy and simple.*

My Dear Daughter,

I love you Dearly and Greatly. I love you with all my heart. Don't give up. Rise up!

*Rise up and reach for all that is there for you.*

So, My Daughter,

Go in peace, love and understanding and don't depart from my words. I love you and you are very special to me. Let my love shine through, then all will know who you are and also know me.

*Don't give up on love.*

Oh, My Daughter,

There is so much that you need to learn, but all in good time. You are doing just fine and I am proud of your efforts to become who you are. So, go in peace and love and the rest will follow you.

And remember, all that the power is: You are.

*The Power of Love is accessible all the time.*

Forever loving you my dear daughter, forever loving you. I wrap my heart around you all the time. Love to you my Princess, love to you.

Divine Mother

*The Divine Mother's Love is wrapped all around us.*

This is just one part of your life that makes you sad. Think of all the other things that make you glad. You are caught up with a deep love for someone who may or may not feel the same way about you.

*There is more than one part of our lives we can focus on.*

My Daughter,

I love and honour your divinity, why don't you do the same?

Mother...

*Our Divinity is our blessedness and love from the universe.*

# Shine Your Light

# Shine Your Light

Shine your light on me dear Mother.

Shine your light on me.

Make the whole world see you shine.

Oh, shine your light on me dear Mother.

Shine so brightly, clear and pure.

In the heavens and down below.

Shine your light dear Mother.

So passing souls may find their way.

Guide them on their way.

Light your lamp for me.

Oh Glorious Mother of Old.

Shine your light on me.

I feel you, now let me glow.

And, so It Is...

*Alpha*

My Dear Daughter,

You are my precious diamond, a precious stone that is yet to be found. You are to be treasured and loved because there is no one else like you. So, shine your light, shine it bright for all to see.

*My Spirit is a reflection of the light within me.*

I love you my daughter, all you need to do is love you. Love who you are, faults and all and don't let anyone dim your light because in the dark you cannot see who you are or where you are going.

So, shine, shine like a star that you are.

*The path will always be lit for you.*

Peace be with you, my daughter. Peace be with you. The ancestors are here for you to call upon at any time that you see fit. But one thing you must always do is to stay in the light. Stay in the light my daughter.

Stay in the light and Shine!

*The light is your source of power.*

I love you, my daughter. I love you, don't forget that. I will always be here to guide you and to love you. Hold yourself up, not down. Aim high at all times. Give yourself the strength that I have given you.

*Hold on to the love of The Divine Mother.*

My Daughter,

You have been having difficulties with another relationship but don't worry my child: all will come right in the end. As long as you shine my light, then all will know who you are.

If it blinds them or makes them glow, well, you have made it known who I Am.

*The love you are looking for can be found in you.*

# Pray

# Pray

Holy Mother and Father,

I have come to you tonight in love peace, joy and happiness.

I know that you are love, so I am love.

I know that you are peace, so I am peace.

I know that you are happiness,

So, I am happy.

Oh, Merciful Mother and Father,

I love you both for abundantly fulfilling my needs.

And, so it Is...

*Alpha*

My Darling Daughter,

Don't despair. I love you and honour you. There is nothing in your life that is not supposed to be. Hear me, my daughter. You are loved greatly by all who know you here on earth and up in the realm of love.

*Don't hold on to the past — cling to the future.*

My Dear Daughter,

Do not despair, help will come to you as you need it and it will be given to you.

*Prayer is a necessary way to heal.*

All that you need to do is ask. Yes, ask for the road to clear and your path will become open for you to walk through.

*Ask for what you need.*

Don't give up on life my darling daughter, just be who you are.

*Call on The Divine Mother for all your needs.*

# To Thyself Be True

Dear Divine Mother and Holy Father,

Last night, I felt your presence and your love. This was very scary for me to know how much love you really have for me and care for me and how Divine I am.

*Oh Mother, teach me to be like you. To love myself in the way that you love me and care for me and the way that you honour me. Teach me how to trust you and learn how to trust myself, to have faith in myself the way you have faith in me.*

*Oh, Glorious Mother who sits so high on her throne, I want to sit with you as your daughter of Love, your daughter of Divinity. In my stillness, talk to me, show me, guide me, command me to listen and follow your ways to uplift myself in a spiritual state always and forever,*

One Love Mother. One Love Father.

Your Daughter of Love

My Dear Daughter,

Hear yourself speak. I love you even when you don't love yourself and even when you don't hear me!

*The clutter in our minds makes it difficult to hear.*

My Dear Daughter,

You are entering a phase of life, a process. You have to overcome the obstacles on the mountain for your own good. These obstacles are there to strengthen you, to guide you and to build you up.

*The journey of life is forever changing.*

Don't despair my daughter, I will always be there guiding you, protecting you and knowing before you even know what you are going to do. Don't despair my daughter, I love you and honour you. I adore you.

*When life is tough, know that The Divine Mother will always be there for you.*

So, things did not work out. Stop beating up on yourself because it did not work out. It was not meant to be. If it was then it would have been granted.

*When things don't go the way you want,*

*there is always another path to walk.*

You can't control life; life is as free as the bird. You just live and let the world around you do the same. You can't control what happens; it is not your concern.

Your concern is You.

*The choice is always yours to make.*

Do what is needed my daughter, in your own little world that you have made for yourself. In your world, it is how you choose to live it, to give it and to get it. So, therefore my daughter, it is all up to you.

*The journey through life is yours to create.*

Do not try to interfere with anyone else's world or you will get lost without a guide.

*I am be-in with the Spirit of the Divine Mother within me.*

Just be yourself, my daughter, and I will do the rest. Truth is what you need. Courage is what you need. Just believe in yourself and the rest will take care of itself.

One Love, my daughter…

*We must have the courage and the strength to be who we are.*

My Dear Daughter,

You have all these qualities yourself and you have the friend that you have always wanted in Me! You don't have to look on the physical, look within the spiritual for all those things and they will come to you bit by bit.

*Life is a process that keeps unfolding like*

*the unwrapping of a present.*

Don't despair my daughter, I know you are going through a rough time but don't despair. All will be well with you. You are passing through a phase and there are things you must learn before you can go onto the next one.

Live in hope of your dreams, whatever they may be and you will see the results.

*Let your dreams be your guide.*

My Daughter,

I love you; I respect you and honour you. Go in peace now in the love that I have bestowed on you. Go in peace my love. Go in peace.

*Step by step is the only action you need to take.*

# Divine Father

Dear Father,

I want to talk to you about a lot of things but the first major question that I want to ask, I know you already know, but it's for me to proclaim it.

Oh, Mighty Father the Omnipotent, the all-Knowing, the all-wise. I wish to, or shall I say, I want to communicate with you.

I want to get to know you. I want to love you in the way you deserve to be loved. My Holy Spirit needs to connect my mind, thoughts and soul.

Holy Father, who are you? Where are you? Are you hiding from me? I need you every second of the day. Oh Father, where are you? Who are you?

I need to know; I need to know.

I am learning more and more each day but what about you? I need to learn more about you. What would you have me do?

Oh Divine, All Powerful one, what will you have me do?

My Dear Child,

I am here. I am with you now! I don't leave my children unattended. Your Ancestors and the Heavenly spirits are all here for our children's glory.

*Lift up yourself to feel the spirit of your Ancestors.*

So, my Dear Daughter, hold up your head high, be filled with my spirit, hold on tight to my love and you will always feel me.

Yes! Feel me.

*Feel the love that the Divine Father has bestowed on you.*

How do you know me? You feel me, you do not see me. I am your image. Don't look for me outside of yourself.

*Don't look outside of yourself, the Divine is within you.*

I am within you, there is no image that shows me apart from you. Yes, I can't be seen by your outwards eyes. I can only be seen as God from within you.

*Let your Divinity flow through you.*

I am all around you: the air you breathe, the trees, the birds, I am the infinite power of all...

So, you see My Queen, I am always with you... It is you that is not with me.

*We are never alone.*

# Darkness and Light

# Darkness

I'm in a cloud.

I'm in a bubble.

Oh boy, am I in trouble.

I'm in a rut.

I'm well and truly caught.

When will these feelings go?

Feelings of sadness.

Feelings of anxiety.

Feelings of not knowing.

I'm in a conflict with myself.

Right, left, yes, no, go, stay?

Peace brings me out of my darkness.

Oh feelings, let there be peace.

Peace in my heart.

Let there be light.

*Alpha*

Ask for the light to open the way for you. Pray for understanding and forgiveness of your situation.

If you dearly and clearly wish this to change, then speak to me alone and ask for the light to shine through the darkness.

*When in the darkness of life, the light is always there.*

My Dear Daughter,

You have the opportunity to be pure in what you do. Do not be afraid. People will not laugh at you; they will not sneer at you. Smile, laugh and enjoy your richness, your greatness and your power.

*Your greatness is your power.*

# Clarity

# Clarity

The storm in my mind has quieted down this morning. It is as reckless as I have been within myself.

I have been feeling unwell inside, not knowing whether I am coming, going, or who I am. I have been taken off track. I seem to be looking and doing the things that I am not happy with, hoping that they would make me happy and it has not worked out like that.

I have been left high and dry (as they say), once again not knowing what to do, how to do it and when to do it. I am now seeing, as it unfolds, what I have done to myself. I have opened the same door that I had opened before, hoping that my treasures would have moved in by now, but this was not the case. I looked and looked, fumbled around to find it. I know I have to admit to myself that I was wrong and that the door never held any treasure in there — only confusion.

Now, I have to shut the door permanently and keep it closed as it is not good for me to go searching around for my treasures. My Divine Mother does not hide my treasures. It is there for me to see abundantly and lovingly. Therefore, I must admit to myself that I would always stumble when this is not for my development....

74

My Dear Daughter,

Don't cry, don't be sad. It will be alright. I promise you. Don't give up on life. You have so much to live for.

*Believing in yourself is the secret of success.*

Do not fret, just be happy that you can love. I know that you won't be loved back the way you want, but one day soon it all will be clear to you. You will know. You will feel and you will understand.

So go in peace my daughter, go in peace.

*When the mind does not bring you joy, stop listening.*

My Dear Daughter,

You must pray for clarity. Pray for love and guidance.

You have drifted from my side, my thoughts and my love.

My Dear, you can't go it alone. I am here to guide you. Talk to me, ask me, speak your truth and I will speak mine to you.

*The only thing that we owe ourselves is to ask for help.*

My Daughter, don't forget that I love you. Now don't forget what I have said to you...

Pray for clarity, peace, love and guidance and it will be given to you.

*Purity of the mind is like the crystal clarity of water.*

My Dear Daughter,

You are divine as you are. You are in the mode of be-in who you are. Living, creating and loving all the time. Just remember that all that you wish for and need I will be there for you, you just call on me.

*When you lie to yourself, you fall hard into reality.*

# Faith and *Trust*

# Our Cry

Oh, Holy Mother on High

Lift up our voices and hear our cry.


A cry for pardon from our wrongs

A cry for love when we are not strong.


Holy Mother, give us this day

To find your love in our own special way.

*Alpha*

All I have to say is, don't worry, you are doing fine. You are doing what you should be doing, so don't worry.

Have faith and know that everything will be alright. Know that you will be alright. Just have faith in yourself. If you have faith and trust in yourself then everything will be alright.

*Have faith in yourself even when you feel hopeless.*

Trust in me, my daughter. Trust me and know that everything will be alright. Relax and don't worry. Do what you have to do and everything will be alright.

I love you and know you are a beautiful woman. Just stay in there.

Peace be with you…

*Faith and trust can break down the strongest of walls.*

The best thing for you to do is just relax and meditate about it. Feel what you are saying in your inner being. Feel the emotions of what you are doing and check within yourself. Does it fit?

Does everything balance as it should? Do they match up? Do they all fit together?

*Check within yourself and know that you will find the answer.*

You must watch the mind very carefully as it will spill out things that have been regretted and turn up to confront you. When this happens, it is there for you to throw out and leave it alone. Do not bury it again or it will show itself all over the place.

*Good thoughts are divinely sent.*

Relax my daughter, relax and everything will be alright. All things are as they should be right here, right now. No-one or no- thing can have power over you. So, take this thought with you.

Deal with yourself first and don't rock anybody's boat and you will be fine.

*Know that you can steer your own boat.*

Oh, Glorious Daughter,

You have a lot to learn. But you are willing to learn and that is okay by me. All that I ask of you is that you remember me in all that you do and all that you say.

I will be there guiding you, protecting you and uplifting you.

*Our abundance has always been held in trust.*

My Merciful Daughter,

You are mine and I am yours. I will always love you no matter what. When you get wounded in battle, come to me and I will clean you up. I will mend your wounds with wisdom and understanding, faith, love and peace.

Forever yours... Forever loving...

Divine Mother xxx

*Divine Mothers love will always mend our wounds.*

Oh daughter, you need to have more trust. I know that your trust has been battered by those around you. I am your mother, learn to trust me before you trust others and everything will fall into place.

*In trusting yourself, nothing else matters.*

Stop hiding under the bushel. Come out and play! Have fun and enjoy yourself. Stop this uncertainty. Have you not seen your gifts? Have you not seen the Mother's touch? Why do you still question what you know and feel?

*Our gifts cannot be taken, lost or*
*destroyed; they are within us.*

Just be, just be who you are and what you are. I will be there with you. I will not leave you, but you need to trust me and honour me more in your life.

*The Divine Mother knows who you are.*

Dear Daughter,

This is what I want you to do. Concentrate on me, trust me. And in doing so, I will show you the light. I will show you what your destiny will be. Trust me and you will see.

*The Divine Mother will not let you*
*down, she can only lift you up.*

## Faith and Trust

My daughter I love you and I will not let anything happen to you that I have not destined for you, if you only trust me.

*Your destiny can travel along many roads as*

*long as you stay on the Divine path.*

I love you, my daughter. Go in peace today and remember trust begins with faith and that is what is holding you back.

So go forward Daughter of Zion, go forward.

*Having faith in yourself is trusting yourself.*

# Soul Purpose

Dear Divine Mother,

I am fine, praises to you, Holy One with the Father in great heights of creation.

I wanted to write to you to let you know how much I love you and care about you. I recognise the love and guidance that you have given me. I love the spiritual way in which you enhance my love. Holy Mother, enable me to follow your guidance and recognise the connection that I have with you in spirit. I love and honour you in all that you do in my life. The way that you have helped me deal with my buried pain and unforgotten things that have plagued me through my life.

I thank you for giving me the ability to deal with all my baggage and giving me the support, I needed to do so. It opened things that I had shut down for a long time. As a child, I was unable to release these things because I was stuck in my pain and unable to go beyond what I was feeling. I was able to forgive those who I felt caused my pain and forgive myself for ever thinking that I was to blame for any of it.

I now know that I need to break out of all the heavy baggage in order to travel light to climb the mountain. My bags must be full of love, understanding, peace, joy, happiness, strength, courage, knowledge, forgiveness, clarity, and faith. I know I have come far from where I have started. I have done a lot of soul searching and questioning about myself that I needed to identify, and I have seen the results of shifting from where I am to where I am going.

Holy Mother, I thank you with my soul from within me. As I go on in this life, I would like to get the best out of myself to be the best of my potential and to embrace mankind with the gifts that you have given me to pass on to your children

I love you and will embrace your words and follow your spirit guidance in order to grow. I recognise that I am all that I am, that I am.

Yes, my daughter, I want to tell you how much I love and care about you.

Look after yourself dearly knowing at all times my daughter there is always room for improvement.

*Growth is necessary in all that we do.*

So that's what I am asking you to do to improve yourself. You are so beautiful, loving and caring within, you must look after yourself.

*Know that you are always protected and loved.*

My Dear Daughter,

Your heart is important to me and to you. It is the shell that houses your soul. You need to maintain your good health. Therefore, I will guide you. Just follow the messages I give you and you will see the improvements.

Forever Yours,

Loving always.

Mother.

*Your heart is your gateway to the soul.*

My Darling Daughter,

Yes, you have been with me right from the beginning of time. I have watched and nurtured you for many long days. Your progress has been slow, due to the surrounding of those who did not know that you were my daughter. You have been led astray by some, but I am happy today because you are back with me, your Mother, the Creator of your life.

*We were created to know and love our Divine Mother.*

My Daughter, I have always been there for you but you allowed others to teach you. You listened to them more eagerly than me. You did not acknowledge me, so I left you to a time when you will come to know who you are and who you are to be.

*Our gifts are always on show.*

Great things are awaiting you, my daughter. One of the greatest things that you have is your love and my love within you! It is from here that you must stand; you are born out of love and you are therefore love.

Go in peace.

*All your answers are within you.*

You are going through a change. Don't hold on to the past. Cling to the future. I will always be here. You are my darling Daughter forever.

*Don't live in the past — it has passed and gone forever.*

So, my daughter, you can only do what you think is right; if it is wrong then you will know. It will be clear to you, but you have to do what needs to be done for your own growth, in order to move from where you are.

*Your spirit will guide you on the right path.*

My daughter, you are a peaceful, loveable, joyous, understanding and knowledgeable soul; do not depart from that.

Do not allow others to tell you who you are. You need to show them who you are.

*Knowing yourself, allows others to know who you are.*

# Fear

# Fear

We would no longer Fear

If we could Oh.

But trust Ourselves.


We would no longer have Fear

If we could Just

Understand Ourselves.


If we fear ourselves

We will fear others.


If we love ourselves

We will also love others.


"Glory Be, Up On High."

*Alpha*

My Dear Daughter,

You must not fear yourself. If you don't try, you won't know. Don't give up on trying, you must try and only then can I help you. I want you to try. Only then can others see my glory.

*In life, risks must be taken. It's the only way you can grow.*

You are denying me as well as yourself when you don't try. Believe in yourself like I believe in you. You are Me and I am You!

Divine Mother.

*Don't deny your dreams, it's time for you to create.*

Oh, Divine Daughter,

How can anyone see your divinity if you don't get out there and let your light shine?

*We carry the light of the Divine Mother.*

My daughter, there are qualities that I have bestowed on you to give to others, so let your light shine. I need you to shine your light so that others will know of me.

*We have been given our qualities to shine in the world.*

Oh, My Dear Daughter,

We are waiting for you to take that first step just like a baby. You may stumble but we will be there to pick you up all the time, so don't worry, just do it.

*The challenge in life is to take that first step.*

We love you; you are one of us. So how can you lose? You will always win. We are with you all the way. So come on, my daughter, it starts today.

Mother.

*Only by trying will you know.*

My dear daughter, fear is yourself. You fear your own greatness. You know that there is an all Powerful and all-Knowing energy within you and yet you push it to one side, not allowing it to be who you are.

*Our greatness should never be feared.*

My dear daughter, you have nothing to fear, I promise you. You are life, you must go through the process of life to achieve anything. Don't be afraid dear daughter. Do your Stuff!

Otherwise, you will never know if you could have been who you want to be.

I love you...don't forget.

*Anything you hold onto that does not*
*benefit you will only get in your way.*

Oh, My Daughter,

You are afraid today, that is what is going on. Your fear is that you don't know enough and you can't do enough and you are not worthy.

*We are created whole and complete — we are enough.*

My Dear Daughter,

You are important to me. You need to realise that whoever you are, I love you always. I will always love you, no matter what you do or say.

*Our fear gets in the way of us receiving our gifts.*

My darling daughter, go in peace, love and understanding and know that I am with you and always will be.

*Having Peace, Love and Understanding is a good way to live.*

Do not be afraid of the unknown. I have already taken care of that. Go in peace my darling, go in peace. I Love you and don't forget me or the Ancestors. Go in peace and surrender.

*Fear not the unknown because we already know.*

My Dear Daughter,

Have no fear about yourself or anyone for that matter. Fear blinds what is really there. Just be who you are and the person who you need to be. Have no fear of what anyone is going to do or say and you will find the light shining through.

*Fear keeps us away from the light.*

You cannot fear another, because another is not superior to you. You are all made from one blood. Your journeys may be different but you are all from the same tree.

*We are all branches of one tree.*

Don't worry my daughter, just be who you are in your light and glory and all will be alright with you. You are my lamp, my light, don't let it go out, don't let it fade. Shine, shine your light for all to see for you are my wonderful creative being.

*Fear will keep your mind stuck in bondage.*

# Forgiveness

My Dear Daughter,

You need to forgive yourself. You have not done so. And the pain you feel is the mind not accepting the past.

*Dwelling on the past stops you living in the present.*

You have not been able to feel comfortable with yourself over this matter. You don't know whether your pain is real or unreal. Whether your mind is being truthful or untruthful.

*You will know what is real when you call on the Divine Mother.*

You need to deal with yourself about something that has happened in your past.

Forgive yourself dear daughter. Forgive yourself unconditionally and wholly.

*Forgive yourself, because only you are feeling the pain.*

You will not move from that pain until you forgive yourself. You can't change what has happened but you can change you. Yes, you can change You.

*Forgive yourself, it will move you through the storm.*

People will always say things with or without meaning, but if you have an understanding of self, then these are just words and you do not have to own them.

*Understand self first; others' opinions*
*have nothing to do with you.*

By holding on to it, you are holding on to your grief. Let it go my daughter, this is just the beginning.

*Oh, my dear daughter, let it go.*

More will come your way through happier times and enjoyable ways. Let it go now my daughter. Forgive yourself and forgive those that trespassed against you.

Forever and ever - I Am.

*It is time for forgiveness and healing.*

# The *mystic* Breeze

# The Mystic Breeze

When you need a voice,
Call me.

When you need help,
shout for me.

When you need peace within you,
I will calm you.

When you need love,
I will embrace you.

When you need understanding,
I will guide you.

When you need knowledge,
I will teach you.

When you need joy,
I will praise and uplift you.

I Am...

*Alpha*

My daughter, my daughter, do not distress yourself. I am here with you and will always be. Yes, you are in a maze, but don't be afraid, all will be well with you.

*There is always a way out of a maze — let*
*The Divine Mother guide you.*

You are...

Divine

Loving

Giving

Understanding

All-Knowing

All wise


That's who you are.


Now, don't ever forget this. Repeat them to yourself every day
and you will see the difference.


*Sometimes you just need to acknowledge the*

*spirit and the attributes that you have.*

My Dear Daughter,

You are focusing on your bad points far too much and too long. Hear this! You are a beautiful, honest, skilful, gentle, lovable, understanding, intelligent, and a giving daughter. You have all this within you waiting to come out. Why do you hide the gifts that I have given you?

*Our uniqueness is our gift from the Divine Realm.*

Don't be afraid of the gifts that I have given you. You are perfect in my sight. You are wonderful, creative and growing. There is no reason for you to be otherwise. Go about your daily life with this knowledge and you will always be peaceful.

*What would happen if our gifts were opened?*

Oh, my daughter, I can't begin to tell you how much you are loved and admired by those who know you. Now get up! And love and admire yourself.

*Self-love and care bring joy to the Divine Mother's heart.*

You are wonderful and giving and loving. Don't depart from these words, the rest will take care of itself. I am your Divine Mother. Trust me, oh daughter, trust me and you will see the difference. I promise you.

*Go with the flow of life — go in peace.*

Go in peace my daughter, you are part of the universe. The world needs you, that's why you are here.

Love, love, love — that's all you need.

Peace be with you.

*You were meant to be here. This is your time.*

Oh, Dear, Dear Daughter,

I love you so much. I love you dear daughter, unconditionally. You are my child; you are growing and I will always be there for you when you need me.

*The love of the Divine Mother cannot be measured.*

Open up your arms my daughter and embrace us to your chest. You are our child of the universe, so you will get no less than what you have asked for.

*Ask for what is yours.*

All you have to do is ask and it will be granted unto you. Yes, we know when things have not been okay with you. But we give you the right to choose which way you want to go.

*The choice is always yours to choose where you want to go.*

Whenever your choice does not make you happy, you just call out our names and we will be there for you.

*Our choices are not fixed forever. Live and seek the ones that give you joy.*

Don't look back, look forward all the time. What is done is done. Just know that everything will be alright. Peace be with you my daughter, go in peace and all will be well.

*Don't look back on your mistakes; look forward to your successes.*

My dear daughter, what more can you do that you have not already done? How much more time and energy are you going to spend on this one?

There is nothing left for you to do but to surrender all of this unto me and your Father to deal with that's all you have to do.

*Don't waste time trying to figure things out — the Divine Mother and Father have the answer.*

My Holy Daughter, have the faith to trust and believe that we will take your situation and circumstances in our deepest heart and give you the perfect solutions for you. Just for you.

*There is a perfect solution in all things.*

You know that all good things come to those who wait. Yes, I know you think you have been waiting for a long time, but in your time only. Our time is different from yours. All will be revealed when the time is right.

*Time cannot be measured; everything comes in The Divine's time.*

Now surrender all your fears and worries about this situation and anything else that you wish, and we will take care of it.

Surrender is the key to your happiness. Just surrender it all unto us and we will do the rest.

*You have to believe it to receive it.*

# Through Thy name

# Through Thy Name

Through Thy Name

Our Beloved Most Glorious

Mother and Father

Within Thy Words of Love.

Uplift Our Souls

To Thy Breast.

Uplift Our Hearts

To Thy Chest.


Heavenly Graces and Blessings is Given to Us

Abundantly and Unselfishly

To Your Children of Love.

*Alpha*

The spirit world and your spirit guide know what you need even before you ask. So go quietly and in peace my darling daughter. All is well in your world. There is nothing that you need that you don't already have.

*Everything you need has already been packed.*

We love you so dearly. Don't fret and worry anymore. We will take good care of you. We cherish and love you and will see that things do not befall you. We know what is in your heart. We hear it every day.

*Good thoughts will bring good things.*

So, continue to be the love that we have created you to be. Move on my Darling do...and be! Just be! You are a child of the universe, you have a right to be here amongst the stars, moon and the sun.

Love to you, my daughter. All our love, forever.

And, so it is...

*Time has no time for the hasty. Everything has it's perfect timing.*

My Dear Daughter,

In this life, you need to take all the things that make you a whole and a complete person.

Anything that does not make you feel this way needs to be dropped and got rid of.

*A heavy heart is difficult to carry.*

You need to know and feel love; you need to understand and be understood. You need knowledge and to be knowledgeable. All these things and more you will need.

*The clutter in our minds makes it difficult to find treasures.*

On your journey, you don't need to carry anyone with you. All the people you need, you will meet on the way for that time and for that moment. They will bring to you what you need. Anything you leave behind is what you don't need.

Peace and love my daughter.

*You don't need to bring anything on your journey, all your needs will be taken care of*

# Reflections

# Reflections

Tonight, I looked back on the morning pages I had written. Fear, anxiety, and low self-esteem were my emotions. My fight. I know that these feelings I had at the time were the reasons not to move and to stay in my comfort zone. However, this was challenged by my inner being. And one by one, each of my emotions had to be dealt with.

I've grown, yes, I can look at these feelings now. I know when they are there. I know when self is being compromised.

Therefore, I have to recognise my state of being was a true inspiration.

I am inspired by just be-in.

I am inspired by self and I am inspired by The Divine Mother within me.

And, so it is...

# Bird Song

The night bird came on a visit

To see me.

Come, come to your land, the bird cries out,

I have beautiful things to show

It's a land of paradise.


So, I leapt and left my bed

To follow the big bird and listened

To what they said.


There's a land that I will take you,

It's far away.

Not many have been there

It's only for the chosen.


I can't tell you what or why,

I've been sent to take you high above and let you fly.


This land is your Treasure Hunt

It's only hidden from your sight,

And not from your view.


Many have been, and many have found

What it is they are looking for.


This is your chance my chosen one.

To find your hidden treasure.

Your treasures are waiting just for you

No one can take them

They belong to you.


So, hurry my chosen one

Do not delay, your treasure awaits


When you have found what you have sought

The gods will cherish your spirt and your thoughts


Chosen one, it's your day

To honour yourself in the blessing

It's not disguised but open for you
Good luck and blessings to you
Your faith will secure it for you.

I will leave you now, oh chosen one
They wait for your visit, don't tarry
They are waiting.

Goodbye oh chosen one
Say hello to the mightier ones
I must now go to another land
To assist in the treasure of another one.

*Alpha*

# Acknowledgements

I'm grateful for all of the help and encouragement I've received while creating this book. Receiving so much from everyone who has joined me on this journey has been incredibly beautiful and heart-warming.

First and foremost, I want to thank and acknowledge My Divine Mother, who has guided me in every way with her spiritual energy and love. I love you; I love you; I love you for making all things possible.

To my Mother, who is resting in high places, I consider myself fortunate to have been your daughter. Because there would not have been... if it hadn't been for your strength, courage, determination, and laughter. Thank you

To my children, who have supported me throughout this creative and spiritual writing. The re-writing, drafts and re-drafts; the sighs, chuckles, and encouragement have helped me along the road. Even when I needed to take a break for rest and thought, the love, support, and wisdom were always there.

To Royston John, who sparked the idea for this book. For giving me the opportunity to see what was there in front of me and bringing to my attention everything that was conceivable and divine.

To Eva Andrea Ditlefsen, my 'Midwife,' who emerged out of nowhere to assist me in giving birth to this book and assisting me in releasing this book at the correct time. Your spiritual wisdom and warmth have helped me to persevere through the difficulties of this spiritual journey.

To Sis Dr Sandra Richards, whose moving preface and testimonial filled me with thanks and admiration for the conscientiousness with which she approached this task. My sister, I Salute You.

To Niya and Sheba, for showing up in my life at the appropriate moment with the right gifts to help me finish this book. Your advice and encouragement have been invaluable to me. Thank you very much.

Finally, to all the divine women reading this book, may your hearts be moved by The Divine Mother's Messages. It's time to claim your divinity.

# About the Author

Imagine that you're meeting Dee, in her flourishing garden. With a burst of heartfelt laughter, she invites you to come and sit with her near the pink roses. The sun is reflected in her bright yellow headscarf, as she leans over and serves you a glass of freshly made carrot juice. A pile of well-read books decorates the wooden table — you recognize self-development, spirituality, poetry and classics, books on history and religion.

Now, the talk goes to all the things she loves, and she shares with you her love for her work as a Life Coach, Teacher, and Mentor. Her passion for helping others to more well-being, clarity, and playing their own tune, has unfolded like the roses by the table. One-on-one coaching, workshops across borders and ages, business events, vision board events — just to mention a few of her talents.

Dee takes a sip of her juice and shares how, after years of teaching, her love for children still inspires her work. Now she also coaches and supports young people to find their own sound. She then turns the conversation to hear all about what makes your heart sing.

You end up hanging out all afternoon. There's a softness and warmth emanating from her whole being that makes you feel safe and inspired. When you say goodbye, Dee heads on to meet her beloved children and grandchildren for family dinner. And you feel like you just got a new best friend.

🌐 www.messagesfromdivinemother.com
🌐 www.deebuchanan.co.uk
📷 messagesfromdivinemother

Printed and bound by CPI Group (UK) Ltd, Croydon, CR0 4YY